A
MOMENT
IN TIME

ADRIAN CORDERO

WRITERS REPUBLIC L.L.C.
515 Summit Ave. Unit R1
Union City, NJ 07087, USA

Website: *www.writersrepublic.com*
Hotline: *1-877-656-6838*
Email: *info@writersrepublic.com*

Ordering Information:
Quantity sales. Special discounts are available on quantity purchases by corporations, associations, and others. For details, contact the publisher at the address above.

Library of Congress Control Number: 2020908874
ISBN-13:   978-1-64620-369-7   [Paperback Edition]
                     978-1-64620-370-3   [Digital Edition]

Rev. date: 05/12/2020

First of all I would like to thank you for buying my book.

I would like to dedicate this book to a few close person's whom were my inspiration and whom I actually wrote these poems to and for.

First of all, my son's mother, Nancy A. Martinez, is whom I would like to dedicate and give gratitude for this book. Although some of the poems she did like and some she was hesitant but I still want to mention her since our love we had was what started as puppy love and years later matured into something bigger and from that love our son Michael Adrian Cordero was born. Many poems I wrote to Nancy and even though a lot she didn't read but they are in this book.

The Second person I'd like to dedicate this book is to Erika Pulido. We met later after high school and online via Facebook. Since meeting her I fell quickly in love with her and I've been even more inspired to write her poems and show her my affectionate side. Leaving her little notes in her car door for her to read after she got off work. Loved being by her side and in many ways she inspired me to write her many love poems and a deep appreciation of her and her gorgeous body.

I also want to dedicate and give respects to my late father whom unfortunately passed away on July 3rd, 2019. When he was still alive and I told him I wanted to write a book of poems and he gave me a green light. Well, here it is father, thank you, wish you could have seen it. R.I.P Jesus M Cordero. We love you and miss you.

Lastly I want to thank everyone else that contributed in me to getting to this point. I have too many to mention but Canutillo Class of 95 - 97. Thanks too to my daughters mom, Maria Veronica Cordero and my two lovely daughters, Maria Vanessa Cordero and Dyanne Victoria Cordero for also being my inspiration.

Evil is what I deeply feel,
Spelled love from ur souls reflection,
Our feelings intensify w every min,
Abyss of filled w deep thoughts,
Nurturing and pampering us selves,
Hugging your thoughts,
Seeing your loving breath saying I luv u,
Longing for minutes to feel your touch,
You complete me to the neutron,
And create that big spark that ignites,
Positivism will always be and our luvin.

Words of love when words from you,
Quiver deep down to my soul and through,
My awaiting heart catches them and holds them,
Only thin energy from these words escape em'
Knowledge of thy mere presence in this world,
Is divine to my heart, mind and soul,
My soul had built a wall around my heart,
To which some have journeyed to and failed,
But it seems that your sweet love has tapped,
The outer wall of my heart and has been heard,
But my heart's ears deceit my own heart,
For thy love is not being heard on the other side,
Thy love has found the door to my heart,
Your tender loving heart has without resistance floated in,
Thy heart's words are being heard loud and clear,
My longing is being lovingly filled by thy words,
After ages, our long awaited hearts,
Are talking together regardless of miles apart. (Erika)

Deep peace brings intense love
Thorough specified combed feelings entice,
Love making to cell level and neutron create dub,
Energy enticifies potently with friction and dam nice,
Universe turns with destiny, time, wish with thee and not sub.

You give me butterflies in thy tummy when I hear your voice,
Thou sight is sight for sore eyes and feel blessed for thee,
Feeling a warm loving feeling in center of chest w no noise,
History of delf from years of past and though ur not w me,
Destiny prewritten, voices spoken, thoughts embraced,
Actions marked, love upwirling and emotions deeply felt,
Sweet brown sugar skin to thy eye titillates enhanced,
Curvy natural signatures of thou body make mind melt,
Self would made thou a Queen and thy would thou King,
For beginning feel of strong of feelings for thou.(Erika)

Sentiment is deep red in part of thee,
Sensation vibrates intensely through aura,
Colors dark yet blinding of love and nurturing,
Essence binding to thou w no resistance nor coma,
Souls communicate via thin line of space unseen,
Memories reenact past of thus and for told,
Symphony plays notes of equilibrium of keen,
Time fading into and developing w/o ur hold,
Strong emotions linger yet passed and unattached,
Life has shown lessons and of learned,
Thou different and self as wild flower unscratched.

Sleep is escape from realness,
Frustration increments as time passes,
Wars fought w many wounded,
Running through halls and doors get closed,
Inspiration and commitment are strong,
Got back on feet to look forward w none among,
Feeling distressed but not beaten,
Journey rough as f but clearly mistaken,
Eyes yet to see path of tree and seed,
In the end promise be, Sun shall help grow seed in need.

Breathed of thy soul in deeply,
Mesmerized was your womanly scent,
Intriguing your sexy voice luvin happily,
Simply knowing thou was with thee was heaven sent,
Thy vibe was infused to thee as soul to body,
Mental shrine of built for thee of had,
Mind daily was in clouds with thou without parody,
Body worshiped as temple as God intended own beauty,
Thy love and everything embedded in thee deeply w no end,
Till end of time will be within thee as no delete exists

Black curly hair moves in delicacy,
Hips provocatively mesmerize thy eye,
Lips massage so tenderly in intimacy,
Skin so soft to the touch is tasty to my,
Eyes dark of color titillate to deep notion,
Your motion is grand endeavor in bed,
Personality instigates in all situation,
Hands gentle and pro as a thoroughbred,
Smile opens inner window to self of bliss,
Curves be like a switch and provoke,
Activity commences without a miss.(Erika)

Breathed out sweet loving words to thee,
Eager ears responded and listening willingly,
Sweet voice symphony to thy self with glee,
Seductive slow rhythmic rainy night enticingly,
Called to listen to mesmerizing tone of thy voice,
Words interchanged lethargically yet lovingly,
Tone was felt deeply as a root in dirt n no noise,
Feeling with great deep intent and knowingly,
Accepted thy feelings and tone with great Poise.

With these words I close my eyes,
For better days shall come to see,
Thy seed shall soon be also with thee,
Major triumphs be accomplished,
Deep sorrows put to rest and in past,
Gloomy days shall be no more,
As negative entity been removed,
A new and pure life lies ahead,
Destiny will be and all 3 seeds will be,
Protected under eagles wings of thee.

Words of sweet love w despair,
Gave me true sweet longed hope,
Took My Breath Away so lovingly,
Gave me intense butterflies in stomach,
Realigned my vision and perspective in life.. I love you (Erika)

Heart is loved and un withered,
Feelings cooked in recipe,
Blood divined into self,
Soul is deeply and heavenly pampered,
A big smile is shown as gratitude,
Self sacrificed and give thy life 2 u.

Heart pumps intense blood,
Veins carry deep feeling,
Soul is moved in surreal thought,
Feeling of love chilling like a villain,
Immensity of thyself engulfs me,
Yet pampers and divines thee.

Deep red colored stem of rose,
Blood flows freely and raging,
Emotions hysterical and high dose,
Soul feels, heals and not aging.

Grew up constructing her characteristics,
Met her unknowingly in early yrs profound,
Years passed, uncharted territory w basics,
Pain and numbness was part of life,
Found her once again in destiny of path,
Self used to uncharted demeaning,
Her was heavenly and self not knew,
Worshipped daily and not acknowledged
Heart saw and felt deeply inner soul
Time and destiny unfolded and she gone.

Red rose bright as blood,
Thorn long pointy as its mood,
Chlorophyll fills it's veins,
It's green color knows no pains,
Withstands sun's uv rays,
Water flows through its veins,
Dirt nourishes w nutrients,
It's soul virgin w/o constituents,
As male/female mating quotients,
Seed is born and grows from rose.

Words as double edge razor,
Either way heard will cut deep,
Blood will spew and pain endure,
Breath will quicken and heart keep,
Raging emotions circle aura of self,
Bright light of above shines blinding,
Healing of wounds from inner soul,
Butterfly out of cage and unwinding,
Sun is at dusk as soul mate waking.

Tone of thy words felt deeply with color,
Breath heard with intent and not sour,
Vibe was clear and with depth not cognito,
Eyes pierced through fog and reached their destino. Xo

Am with a knot of emotional feelings in my throat,
Which have accumulated over time and will not float,
Love, hate, longing, sadness and happiness are mixed in,
Different circumstances have caused them and from within,
I see hope of finally releasing this knot out and free,
From within in me and out into this chaotic world where it should be,
There is a tender and loving voice which I miss and hold so dear,
Which to my believing would cause a relief to this that I fear,
And end this battle that happens from within this knot I feel,
To bring a new chapter of my life and conquest to thee,
Which I would love to share with you and me.

Your hair is expression of thyself,
Your personality is unique and feisty but delf,
Selfishness is not in your vocabulary nor is greed,
You care for others and your thoughts are unseen,
But are widely known by closeness and by heaven,
Your ego does not exceed u nor controls you,
You are God sent and angel driven in the path placed before you,
You carry on day by day changing peoples live in the eyes of you,
For God is in all of us.. and You/We are in God ....

Your words are like red to a rose petal,
The sound of your breath is like polish on metal,
You bring shine to dullness and love to bitterness,
You are worth a million women and are a Heirs,
Your womanly scent is the nectar of example to followers,
Pride is of descent, integrity and prosperous to hers,
Words can only say so much for thy self is a temple to others. (Nancy)

Life's expressions and attitudes have surely impressed,
Doubt's raised and destiny proven, words said & listened,
Nervousness felt intensely, love longed and felt abyssly,
World changes its axis as some people have X's,
New horizon's are appearing regardless of uneasiness,
Optimism in veins and heart, regardless that we're apart,
River had been flowing vigorously for some time,
Different currents have passed as well from time 2 time,
Feelings have ridden like a roller coaster many times,
Once this boat sees the long awaited shore,
I will never leave it and will fight for what is true,
Many fights I've battled throughout years,
Many tears shed, emotions torn and numbed,
This one i will overcome and make us true.
When two life entities love each other, they have all the
right to be together Regardless of obstacles (Nancy)

Has eyes and mind of roses divine thee,
Sweet berry candle scent fills the room,
Energy derived from love and soul deep within,
White little feet selfies exploring world around his,
Warm loving air surrounds objects and is norm,
Expressions rudimentary yet sweet as honey n cute as can be,
Honey colored hair with pearl smile on face of angel,
In due time destiny will cross and be in life of thee as pure bliss.

Deep red colored stem of rose,
Blood flows freely and raging,
Emotions hysterical and high dose,
Soul feels, heals and not aging.

Dreamed as a teenager of my perfect woman,
Grew up constructing her characteristics,
Met her unknowingly in early yrs profound,
Years passed, uncharted territory w basics,
Pain and numbness was part of life,
Found her once again in destiny of path,
Self used to uncharted demeaning,
Her was heavenly and self not knew,
Worshipped daily and not acknowledged
Heart saw and felt deeply inner soul
Time and destiny unfolded and she gone.

Red rose bright as blood,
Thorn long pointy as its mood,
Chlorophyll fills it's veins,
It's green color knows no pains,
Withstands sun's uv rays,
Water flows through its veins,
Dirt nourishes w nutrients,
It's soul virgin w/o constituents,
As male/female mating quotients,
Seed is born and grows from rose.

Words as double edge razor,
Either way heard will cut deep,
Blood will spew and pain endure,
Breath will quicken and heart keep,
Raging emotions circle aura of self,
Bright light of above shines blinding,
Healing of wounds from inner soul,
butterfly out of cage and unwinding,
Sun is at dusk as soul mate waking.

Your thoughts spoke loudly,
Hindered in the emotion,
Ravished by winds love,
Tethered by blind sight,
Nurtured by my inner-self,
Pampered vigorously,
Yet not inconvenienced,
Rather nicely take care of,
Inner orgasmic abyss felt,
Heavens opened in near feeling,
Toes curled, eyes rolled,
Hands squeezed endlessly,
Then just rode the endless waves.

Abyss feeling of hate and rage evolved,
Years ago that feeling didn't exist as developed,
Seems its a dormant volcano stirring inner-self,
Intensity of rage to many extreme levels of existence,
Hatred thought to many extremes and felt to core,
Wanting to desperately erupt and cause havoc,
Many years passed and wished for thy existence deleted,
Feelings, thoughts, taste and anything to do with thee,
Boils and causes turmoil within and yet mind somehow,
Creates equilibrium within thou regardless of pressure,
Many eons it seems of such pain and endurance,
The positive and negative charge has exploded,
Chaos has commenced and anarchy is instigated,
Time will tell and destiny will decide fate,
Regardless of self implosion,
Inner peace and happiness will emerge without thee,
And a new chapter will begin,
With no looking back.

Your words massaged me,
Your breath invigorated me,
Your presence next to me ignites,
The stars will never shine brighter than ur eyes,
Your soul will always be intense to me as our existence,
Having hard time finding words to describe what I feel,
For your mere existence in this lifetime,
Has me mesmerized and in awe,
And am DAM glad that we found each other,
Regardless our previous obstacles.

Intensity grows as suspense rises,
Longing is an abyss with tears,
Ocean of deep blue feelings,
Dolphins mix the good n bad,
Deep currents remind of self,
Your love is in the molecules,
My loving rage longs for you,
I see you in a far distance,
My anxiety misses u,
Every breath has your vowel,
Fish swim in symphony 4 u,
We bring equilibrium to our earth,
With every second comes intensity,
With every wave comes serenity,
I need you and i miss you so,
A clock needs sprockets to tick,
And you are my 1 & only chick,
Destiny is unfolding in due time,
I know 4 a fact that U Will B Mine.

Sweet R&B playing smoothly,
The suave of your hair sways,
Gently touching your side arm,
Breath tightens up as we kiss,
Night stars become our lights
Rythm kicks in and tempo up,
High notes sound crisp n loud,
Great Symphony is made & njoyed,
I'm playing your G in D minor,
End result is total bliss in harmony.

I deeply breathed your love,
Enjoyed it's loving taste,
Savored it so dearly,
Longing for such exquisite smell,
Sadly I had to exhale,
And let the world enjoy that special breath,
Your words nurture my ears,
And soul to the neuron,
Dam.... how much I've longed for u..

The red sparrow flinched at it's mate,
Breeze flowed it's breath naturally,
Woodpecker pecked vigorously,
Roses petal invigorates with love,
Our energy vibrates so intense measured as an earthquake,
We speak as if we've known each other for lifetimes, not years.
Destiny shall unfold and road paved,
Every step and word spoken,
Will see as a dejavu... for we were predestined.

Sweet memories I have of you,
Holding you at birth in my arms,
Tears rolled gently as I saw u first,
Hearing your sweet voice crying,
Seeing your new tears flow,
You in a new world and I there 2 greet u,
You are and always will be my treasure,
Your my one and my only son,
Time will come when I will see you again,
Blood remembers and sticks to,
Just wish I could hold you now,
And be there with you, us... love u,
Mi Cachorro. (Michael)

Deep dark red wine flows rich,
Blood red with your love,
It's smell entices and drunkens,
Spontaneously sexy as wine's red,
Savoring as caviar to tongues taste,
Taste buds go crazy with such delight,
Longed of such intense delicacy,
Profound marinade in self of u,
Dam I longed of such taste,
Deep sigh and glad to breathe,
Ever longing breath of urs.

Your words flow as water,
Taste like gummy bears to me,
Hearing ur thoughts melt me,
Invigorating indeed into abyss of bliss,
Wow....your laughter is medicine,
All perfectly balanced into harmony.
Thank you

Deep breaths taken in anxiety,
Heart is pounding non stop,
Holding back the tears lump in throat,
Rage is at full swing and wanting out,
Destiny will finally unfold and path shown,
Sweet sorrow is deeply felt yet many battles won,
Eventually triumph will be sweet victory,
Storm shall have passed and peace overcome the land,
Love and faith will definitely overcome and prevail,
I shall finally hear thy words spoken,
Presence fully and deeply acknowledged,
And loving entity at last regained..

Breeze flowed through gently,
Caressing my cheek,
Reminded me of your soft touch,
Sun shines brightly on my face,
Such as your loving glance at me,
Birds sing your love song at me,
Leaves slowly fall as our love grows,
Water in the creek flows as our thoughts,
Moons have shined leading me 2 you,
Our auras are strong and bright,
Can only imagine what destiny has in store for us if any.

Time passes and miles ran,
Seasons evolve and dissolve,
Looking for verbs and subjects,
Different inner energy in aura,
Loving bliss fills abyss,
Greater triumphs commencing,
Euphoric state of mind,
Wide open mindness to triumphantness,
Enthusiamastic voyage commenced,
New chapter begun in bliss delight,
Great and awesome endeavors begin!

Sound touches ear and envelopes,
Deep sorrow commencing,
Longing feeling is lingering,
Past reminds of sweet bliss,
Once was and now long gone,
New chapter begun with overlay,
Smoke tainted and whiskey taste,
Caramel skin and black hair miss,
Friday family nights and cards,
Evening stroll and cruising,
Watching airplanes land with bliss,
Enjoyed seeing your happiness,
Tried mending in self and sour,
Ego and pride too overflow,
Best to squander and flee,
Regardless heart still imprinted,
Memories of you will always be,
Hope you realize and change,
Miss you dearly,
However, traveling my path...(Erika)

Sweet sorrow when I bit into air,
Most seeds in burrow cling,
Dirt feels better barefoot,
As love swims freely when no restraint,
Flower and tulip bloom flawlessly,
Ages pass and Picasso pic at view,
To some misconstrued, others art,
Smoke happens with fire,
As lungs use oxygen,
piano talks only if u touch it,
Love is not a piano, but a 2 way street.(Erika)

Sad night reveals with quite storm,
Heavy rain pours as do tears,
Heart slow beating with pain,
Breath shallow with absence,
Soul is rotting every second,
Pain is numb by severed nerves,
Migraines remind me I'm still alive,
Feel like an itch from a mosquito bite,
Cut myself accidentally and didn't feel,
Seems body in shock and numb,
Feeling blood slowly oozing through,
Hard cold floor which I'm lying on concrete,
Ceiling lamp on like a dying candle,
Eyes barely see few feet away,
Last breath seems and sight starts fade,
Body feels cold and body tingles,
White light appears and body no longer,
See my self over my body,
I see my dad behind light and I follow...

Breathed soft water,
And drank wet air,
Felt the smooth air,
Saw the lovely aroma,
Fire was dancing with water,
Love mingled with hate,
Sadness was BFF with joy,
Time exists in self n realm,
Tasted fire as a flickering feather,
Made of hottest pepper,
Poles N & S are opposite and attract,
Yet ur pole is WTF and not for me,
The environment says it all,
And seems it is not meant 2 b.

Thoughts I thought of u,
Thoughts many of u,
Mind of mine full of u,
Mind overflows of u,
Desire to live with thee,
Desire to be with thee,
Desire to breathe ur breath deeply,
To inhale your breath and absorb,
Enjoy your breath deeply,
To have ur breath feed my soul,
To have your voice feed my heart,
Simply having you keeps me alive,
I love u, I need u.(Erika)

A special world for you and me
A special bond one cannot see
It wraps us up in its cocoon
And holds us fiercely in its womb.
Its fingers spread like fine spun gold
Gently nestling us to the fold
Like silken thread it holds us fast
Bonds like this are meant to last.
And though at times a thread may break
A new one forms in its wake
To bind us closer and keep us strong
In a special world, where we belong.
Words can only say so much,
For actions are strong as such,
My love is fierce and will fight for ur love,
Through good and bad times like God's love

Saw a blue Jay fly by and landed,
Feathers big and fluffy full of love,
Jay looks at surroundings,
Wind whispering about his love,
It prepares his nest for possibility,
He's prepared for the quest,
The Jay gives a strong high leap,
And he dives for his destiny..

I dreamed a dream,
Eyes fulfilled,
Imagination ran wild,
Emotion bewildered w love,
Soul pleased and pampered,
Self centered and aimed,
Future is secured,
Destiny finally to be fulfilled

I sent u a letter,
Words u read,
Impression felt deeply,
Many subjects and verbs,
Adjectives scare and entail,
Curvaceous indeed felt,
Newly vision titillates thee,
Destiny unfolding,
Foundation rebuilt,
New era commencing,
Bliss inevitable.(Erika)

Body dropped from hanger,
Noose around neck,
Neck broke clean off from slam,
Body fell to ground,
Head stuck on noose,
Blood squirting every where,
Silence is heard and smiles seen,
Body jerking lasts jerks,
Eyes pupils loosing sight,
Veins draining from pain,
Dark is commencing,
Dark angel seen,
It looks and it goes away,
Even self is not worthy of death,
That even death itself turns away,
Having to have some surgeon sow the body back together
And give blood transfusion cause body won't fucking die,
Keeps living, To feel all the extreme pain and humiliation,
For as long as it'll fucking take...
Lessons many to still be learned.

Eyes are pampered,
Deep breathe taken,
Spur felt and deeply,
Exhilaration exists w abyss,
Love and sadness wallow,
End results entice seeds

Eyes of soul see thee so flourished,
Longing breath awaits ur touch,
Loving voice caresses thy skin,
Seems like eons since last encounter,
Full embrace brings deep bliss,
Enveloped into self deeply as root,
Seeing flower bloom from thou eye,
Soul smiles reflecting from heaven,
Ur words end my sentences,
As subject to predicate,
Sun to moon and sunrise 2 sunset,
Heart beat skips in your presence,
As your voice invigorates,
Window was open and u saw me,
Else is unfolding.(Erika)

I saw a ravishing tulip,
Rare of its kind and exquisite size,
Soul pure and great to tip,
Your loves energy revives,
Destiny is preset and carved,
Itinerary is given to thee,
Actions being lived as saved,
Thoughts, words and breath heave,
Heavenly intense pure love,
That envelopes two entities,
And new life begins.(Erika)

Damn.... the flower petal fell slowly,
The hummingbird flew as usual,
The nectar dripped,
Sun shinning hot and bright,
Cumulus clouds above,
Air is thick and humid
Object in air gets wet
Soul sees and musters,
Ounces to pounds,
Love to breathe,
Earth to seed,
Eyes to sight,
These words read by u,
Felt by others,
New Era began,
And destiny is unfolding.
Time is approaching,
And I will be with you again n 4 ever. 14.1.14.3.23. (Nancy)

I breathe with your scent,
I see of your heart,
I think of your mind,
Treasure everything bout u,
Obsess on ur being,
U attract me in every way,
It's like my mission yet destiny,
To love you like I've never loved before with deep intensity,
To love you like there's no tomorrow,
To do, to tell you everything that comes to my mind cause I don't
know if you or I will be here tomorrow, love you as intensely as I
possibly can and give you my all.. tell u how much I love you and
how much you mean to me. I want you to know that is the reason I
love you like I do. ..because I'm also hungry to love someone as dam
fucking special like you .... deep sigh..... thank you, I love u..(Erika)

CPSIA information can be obtained
at www.ICGtesting.com
Printed in the USA
LVHW090416020620
657199LV00001B/314